Messages of

GRATITUDE

for **Advent** and **Christmas 2021**

Messages of

GRATITUDE

for **Advent** and **Christmas 2021**

3-MINUTE DEVOTIONS

MICHAEL WHITE and **TOM CORCORAN**

AVE MARIA PRESS AVE Notre Dame, Indiana

Founded in 1865, Ave Maria Press is a ministry of the United States Province of Holy Cross.

www.avemariapress.com

Paperback: ISBN-13 978-1-64680-103-9

E-book: ISBN-13 978-1-64680-104-6

Cover and text design by Samantha Watson.

Printed and bound in the United States of America.

Introduction

The Advent and Christmas seasons come with many special traditions. For both of us, watching holiday movies and TV specials ranks high on the list. While we disagree on almost everything else, we do agree on the must-watch status of three classics in particular: *A Christmas Carol* starring Alastair Sim, *A Charlie Brown Christmas*, and our personal favorite, *It's a Wonderful Life*.

Many of you know the story of *It's a Wonderful Life*. George Bailey learns to see how wonderful his life has been by observing what would have become of his friends and family if he had never been born. That difference in perspective changes everything for him. He comes to see his family, his work, and his place in the community as gifts instead of burdens and disappointments. As a result of his change in perspective, he embraces the virtue of gratitude. Clarence, his guardian angel, underlines the value of this attitude when he tells George, "You have been given a great gift."

The word gratitude comes from the Latin word *gratia*, which means grace. Grace is a gift. It is something we receive and not something we can earn. Everything we have is a gift from God, and it is important to stay focused on that. In fact, it can be critically important. There are numerous studies which show that there's no behavior more effective at increasing your happiness and well-being than cultivating and practicing gratitude. In one study, psychologists from the University of California asked a group of participants to keep a simple daily journal. One group was told to write about things they were grateful for, and the other to record their daily disappointment and irritations. After ten weeks, members of both groups were evaluated. Not surprisingly, the group focused on gratitude faired far better by every measurable standard: emotional health, physical health, productivity, and quality of relationships.

Centuries before psychology identified the connection between gratitude and happiness, God's word taught this universal and eternal truth. Psalm 28:7 says, "The LORD is my strength and my shield, in whom my heart trusts. I am helped, so my heart rejoices; with my song I praise him."

Psychology *and* scripture affirm the power of gratitude to bring joy and happiness into our hearts and our homes. Our own experience does too. When we forget to practice gratitude, we can easily lose our perspective on the many gifts God has given us; our vision becomes clouded when it comes to our blessings. That's why we have to bring this matter to prayer.

In this sacred season, when we await the joy of celebrating the coming of the Lord, we present to you this seasonal booklet focused on prayerful gratitude. We hope that it will help you to practice this crucial virtue each day of Advent and through the twelve days of Christmas. As you spend just a few minutes in reflection and prayer each day, may your heart and mind be made ready to receive the many gifts of Christmas, especially the gift of God's only beloved Son who comes to live among us.

Fr. Michael and Tom
Church of the Nativity, Timonium, Maryland

FIRST WEEK

OF ADVENT

Sunday, November 28

The holiday season is here, as we have exactly one month to get ready for Christmas! Over the next month, we will be incredibly busy with parties; buying, wrapping, and sharing gifts; decorating our houses; watching holiday specials; and creating memories for our families. There are so many blessings and good things happening at this time of year that they can start to feel like a burden instead of a blessing at times.

To help you stay focused on the blessings and appreciate your life more fully, we offer this small book of daily spiritual messages. We hope that these three-minute devotions will help you grow a spirit of gratitude and thankfulness. When we lose our sense of gratitude, we lose our joy, our happiness, and our sense of well-being. Ingratitude is incompatible with happiness and hinders our path to knowing and loving God.

....

Pray today that, as you make your many preparations for Christmas, you will grow in gratitude for all the gifts God has given you, especially the gift of his Son.

Monday, November 29

And from Jesus Christ, the faithful witness, the first-born of the dead and ruler of the kings of the earth. To him who loves us and has freed us from our sins by his blood.

—Revelation 1:5

Gratitude begins with recognizing the blessings in our life. Our greatest blessing is Jesus Christ. In the book of Revelation, John reminds us of the blessings and gifts we have in Jesus. He is the faithful witness of God's love. His death on the Cross reminds us that when we turned our back on God, God did not turn his back on us. He remained faithful and sent his Son.

Jesus is the firstborn of the dead. He rose from the dead but is only the first. We, too, will rise when connected to him. We can be grateful that, in Christ, we can conquer death. Jesus loves us and has freed us from our sins by his blood. In Christ, we not only have life after death but also have freedom to live now as God's sons and daughters.

....

Read the verse from Revelation again. Thank Jesus for the many gifts that come from a relationship with him.

Tuesday, November 30

Therefore, we who are receiving the unshakable kingdom should have gratitude, with which we should offer worship pleasing to God in reverence and awe.

—Hebrews 12:28

The kingdom of God lasts forever. It is a kingdom that cannot be shaken or taken away from us. The kingdom of this world will pass away, but God's kingdom lasts forever.

In Jesus, we receive the kingdom of God and all his blessings. While the gifts we have in this world are passing and we will one day lose them all, the riches of God's kingdom cannot be taken away from us.

....

Thank God today for the blessings you have in Jesus Christ. Thank God that you cannot lose them.

Wednesday, December 1

As he was entering a village, ten lepers met [him]. They stood at a distance from him and raised their voice, saying, "Jesus, Master! Have pity on us!" And when he saw them, he said, "Go show yourselves to the priests." As they were going they were cleansed.

—Luke 17:12–14

Luke tells us that Jesus is going on a journey. He enters a village and is met by ten lepers. Lepers had to live on the outskirts of town away from society. When anyone came near them, they were supposed to yell out, "Unclean, unclean" so that people would know to stay away. Instead, these lepers beg Jesus for mercy, and Jesus tells them to go to the priests. As they obey Jesus, following his instruction, they are healed.

Like the lepers in this story, we need Jesus' mercy. Like the lepers, we need Jesus to cleanse us and make us whole. The more we are aware of our need for Jesus and realize our need for his mercy, the more likely it is that we will be able to recognize his blessings.

....

Pray today with the lepers, "Jesus, Master, have pity on me." Say that five to ten times. Then, pray it throughout the day.

Thursday, December 2

And one of them, realizing he had been healed, returned, glorifying God in a loud voice; and he fell at the feet of Jesus and thanked him. He was a Samaritan.

—Luke 17:15–16

Jesus heals ten lepers, but only one of the ten sees that he has been cleansed. Rather than just going on with his life, the man stops and turns back. He praises God and then falls at Jesus' feet as a way to express his gratitude.

The first step of gratitude requires that we see our blessings. The second step is to do what the leper did—turn back or turn our attention to the benefactor or giver of the gift. The third step is to express our gratitude. We can express gratitude to God by simply saying thank you, praising him in song, or falling on our knees in worship as the leper did.

....

Take a moment to reflect on the last twenty-four hours. Recognize the gifts you have received. Turn your attention to God and thank him for them.

Friday, December 3

Jesus said in reply, "Ten were cleansed, were they
not? Where are the other nine? Has none but this
foreigner returned to give thanks to God?" Then
he said to him, "Stand up and go; your faith has
saved you."

—Luke 17:17–19

Jesus cleansed all ten lepers, but only one came
back to him. The Samaritan leper was the only one
who came back to Jesus, and because he returned,
he received more than the others. The other nine
received only physical healing, but the Samaritan
leper also received salvation. He entered into a relationship with Jesus.

When we return to God and thank him for his
gifts, God can do more for us. God gives us gifts
to meet our specific needs. He loves to meet our
needs, but ultimately God gives us gifts so that we
can grow deeper in our relationship with him.

....

Turn your attention to God and thank him for the gifts
you have received from him. Listen to Jesus say, "Rise
and go your way, your faith has saved you."

Saturday, December 4

Psalm 103:1–10

O bless the Lord; my soul!

O bless the LORD; my soul; all my being bless his
holy name!

Bless the LORD, my soul; and do not forget all his
gifts,

Who pardons all your sins, and heals all your ills.

O bless the Lord; my soul!

Who redeems your life from the pit, and crowns
with you mercy and compassion,

Who fills your days with good things, so your youth
is renewed like the eagle's.

O bless the Lord; my soul!

The LORD does righteous deed, brings justice to all
the oppressed.

He made known his ways to Moses, to the Israelites
his deeds.

O bless the Lord; my soul!

Merciful and gracious is the LORD, slow to anger,
abounding in mercy.

He will not accuse, and nurses no lasting anger;

He has not dealt with us as our sins merit, nor
requited us as our wrongs deserve.

O bless the Lord; my soul!

Second Week

OF ADVENT

Sunday, December 5

As we get ready for Christmas during this second week of Advent, we are working on growing in gratitude and appreciating the life God has given us. While ingratitude is incompatible with happiness, grateful people are happy people. Since all of us are on a happiness quest, it makes sense to grow in gratitude.

First, we need to see the blessings and gifts given to us. If we don't see them, then it is impossible to be grateful. Second, we need to turn our attention toward the giver of the gifts. Ultimately, God is the giver of all our blessings. So, to express gratitude, we must turn toward the source of our blessings and give God attention. In all of God's gifts, he wants to build a relationship with us.

Last, we need to express our gratitude. We need to do something in response to the gifts we are given and are grateful to have received. But sometimes this is hard to do. This week, we will be examining obstacles that get in our way of seeing God's blessings and responding to them in gratitude and action.

....

Ask God today to help you see what gets in the way of recognizing his blessings and gifts. Pray for the grace to overcome these obstacles.

Monday, December 6

There will be signs in the sun, the moon, and the stars, and on earth nations will be in dismay, perplexed by the roaring of the sea and the waves. People will die of fright in anticipation of what is coming upon the world, for the powers of the heavens will be shaken.

—Luke 21:25–26

Jesus speaks of a time when "people will die of fright." This is hyperbole. We would say it this way: "I was scared to death" or "He was scared to death." Jesus warns that people will be scared to death when the Temple is destroyed. The foundations of their faith will be shaken because the Temple was the foundation of their faith. It would be a disaster so large that people would be terrified.

We can lose sight of God's blessings when we are facing big problems or going through major changes. We can focus all of our attention on those hardships, and they can come to dominate our thoughts and weigh down our hearts.

....

What major problems or change are you facing now or fear will happen in the future? Confess it to God. Acknowledge it. Ask God for the grace to see beyond the problem and to trust in his mercy and grace.

Tuesday, December 7

And then they will see the Son of Man coming in a cloud with power and great glory. But when these signs begin to happen, stand erect and raise your heads because your redemption is at hand.
—Luke 21:27–28

Jesus describes a time of tribulation when the Temple in Jerusalem will be destroyed. Most people will be terrified, but Jesus says that his followers can have the opposite reaction. They are to stand firm and look toward him because their redemption is coming.

When big problems and major changes hit us, we don't have to be scared. We can instead be grateful and focus our attention on Jesus, who is the Son of Man. The name "Son of Man" communicates both Jesus' humanity and divinity. It means that Jesus knows firsthand our pain and struggles and also has the power to do something about them. Faith is thanking God in advance for working out all things for our good, despite and often through our biggest challenges.

....

Thank God today that whatever major problems or issues you are facing; he is using them for your good.

Wednesday, December 8
Solemnity of
the Immaculate Conception

Beware that your hearts do not become drowsy from carousing and drunkenness and the anxieties of daily life, and that day catch you by surprise.
—Luke 21:34

Big problems can block us from seeing God's blessings, but so can little things. The day-to-day grind of balancing work life and home life, managing anxiety, accomplishing our daily tasks, dealing with frustrating people, and all our other challenges can rob us of gratitude.

Jesus wants us to not allow the daily anxieties of life to rob us of a grateful heart. Do not let these things be a trap. One way we can avoid the ingratitude trap is to remember the blessings behind the burdens. Thank God for both the material goods that make life easier and for the spiritual gifts of Mary, conceived without sin, and all the saints, who are our companions and guides.

....

What are the daily anxieties that rob you of a grateful heart? Through the intercession of Mary, thank God today for the blessings behind the burdens.

Thursday, December 9

Rejoice always. Pray without ceasing. In all circumstances give thanks, for this is the will of God for
you in Christ Jesus.

—1 Thessalonians 5:16–18

Paul tells us clearly of God's will for us. In every single circumstance we are to rejoice, pray, and give thanks to God. God wants us to rejoice, pray, and give thanks because he knows that will give us a better life. If in every circumstance we rejoice, pray, and give thanks to God, we will live a life of value and purpose.

In all circumstances means that, even in our trials and tribulations and struggles, we are to thank God. We don't thank God for the circumstances. We thank God that he is at work in our circumstances.

....

Pray today for the grace to give thanks to God regard-
less of your circumstances. Take a moment to memo-
rize the verse above from 1 Thessalonians so that the
next time the daily anxieties of life take over, the Holy
Spirit can remind you to have an attitude of gratitude.

Friday, December 10

Have no anxiety at all, but in everything, by prayer and petition, with thanksgiving, make your requests known to God. Then the peace of God that surpasses all understanding will guard your hearts and minds in Christ Jesus.

—Philippians 4:6–7

Paul tells us to have no anxiety about life. When our hearts become anxious, we can choose to worry or we can make a better choice. We can turn our attention to our problems, or we can turn our attention to God. We can ask God for help through prayer and petition. We can ask God to act, thanking him because he knows us and hears us and has our best interest in mind.

When we thank God in advance, Paul tells us that we will receive God's peace. It is a peace that surpasses understanding because it is based not on our circumstances but on God's goodness and faithfulness. It is a peace beyond understanding because it guards our hearts from future anxieties.

....

What are you anxious about? Make your requests about the circumstances known to God. Thank God in advance for what he is going to do.

Psalm 98:1–4

Sing to the Lord a new song, for he has done marvelous deeds.

Sing to the LORD a new song,
> for he has done wondrous deeds;
His right hand has won victory for him,
> his holy arm.

Sing to the Lord a new song, for he has done marvelous deeds.

The LORD has made his salvation known:
> in the sight of the nations he has revealed his
> > justice.
He has remembered his kindness and his
> faithfulness
> toward the house of Israel.

Sing to the Lord a new song, for he has done marvelous deeds.

All the ends of the earth have seen
> the salvation by our God.
Sing joyfully to the LORD, all you lands
> break into song; sing praise.

Sing to the Lord a new song, for he has done marvelous deeds.

THIRD WEEK

OF ADVENT

Sunday, December 12

While ingratitude is incompatible with happiness, grateful people are happy people. We have noted that there are steps to gratitude: recognizing our gifts, turning our attention toward the giver, and expressing gratitude.

This week, we invite you to reflect on the people who have been a blessing in your life. Among God's greatest gifts to us are the people who fill our lives. We can thank God for our family members, friends, coworkers, coaches, teachers, and mentors.

....

Thank God today for the people he has placed in your life. This week, ask God to help you recognize those who have blessed you. Ask the Holy Spirit to bring those people to mind frequently and thank God continually.

Monday, December 13

I give thanks to my God at every remembrance of you, praying always with joy in my every prayer for all of you, because of your partnership for the gospel from the first day until now.

—Philippians 1:3–5

Paul thanks God for the Philippians. He says something so beautiful: every time he thinks about them, every time their names are mentioned or they come to mind, he smiles and thanks God for his relationship with them. As he experiences gratitude for the Philippians, he is also filled with joy. Paul reminds us that gratitude and joy, gratitude and happiness, go together.

Are there any people in your life who give you the same reaction? They have been such a blessing in your life that every time you think of them, just the thought of them brings a smile to your face. Just their presence encourages you.

....

Thank God for whoever brings a smile to your face when you think of them. After your prayer, write an email, a text, or an actual letter to let the person know about your prayer of gratitude.

Tuesday, December 14

And this is my prayer: that your love may increase ever more and more in knowledge and every kind of perception, to discern what is of value, so that you may be pure and blameless for the day of Christ, filled with the fruit of righteousness that comes through Jesus Christ for the glory and praise of God.

—Philippians 1:9–11

Paul thanks God for the Philippians, and then he prays for them. He offers a prayer of thanksgiving for them and then a prayer of supplication. Since he had been their spiritual mentor, he prays that their ability to love will multiply with knowledge and discernment.

We can't just treat everyone the same; we have to know each person and discern in each situation what is best, what is most loving. Paul prays that the Philippians will grow in love and in knowing how to love. He prays that they will become more like Christ through the fruits of righteous, which are joy, peace, patience, kindness, goodness, and self-control.

....

Thank God today for someone you have mentored or in whom you have invested time and energy. Thank God for the opportunity to pass on what you know to others. After your prayer, write an email, a text, or an actual letter to let the person know about your prayer of gratitude.

Wednesday, December 15

First, I give thanks to my God through Jesus
Christ for all of you, because your faith is heralded
throughout the world. God is my witness, whom I
serve with my spirit in proclaiming the gospel of his
Son, that I remember you constantly, always asking
in my prayers that somehow by God's will I may at
last find my way clear to come to you.

—Romans 1:8–10

In his letters, Paul regularly thanked God for the
community he addressed. When writing to the
Romans, Paul thanked God for their faith. They
had such a deep faith and trust in God that it was
known throughout the whole world. Paul told the
Roman Christians that he longed to be able to go
to them.

Paul praises the Romans because of their
strong faith. They have inspired many others
throughout the world. Call to mind someone
whose faith has been an inspiration to you. Perhaps
it is your parents who modeled faith for you as a
child. Perhaps it is a member of your small group
or someone who volunteers in a ministry at church.

....

Thank God today for someone who has inspired you
and encouraged you to grow in faith. After your prayer,
write an email, a text, or an actual letter to let the person know about your prayer of gratitude.

Thursday, December 16

What thanksgiving, then, can we render to God for you, for all the joy we feel on your account before God? Night and day we pray beyond measure to see you in person and to remedy the deficiencies of your faith. Now may God himself, our Father, and our Lord Jesus direct our way to you, and may the Lord make you increase and abound in love for one another and for all, just as we have for you, so as to strengthen your hearts, to be blameless in holiness before our God and Father at the coming of our Lord Jesus with all his holy ones.

—1 Thessalonians 3:9–13

Paul writes that he is thankful for the Thessalonians and filled with love for them. He prays that he will be able to come in person to see them so he can remedy their deficiencies in faith. This sounds a bit condescending, but Paul does not intend to condescend. Rather, he wants to come to serve them and give them what they need to grow in faith.

God places people in our lives who challenge us to grow and be the best we can be. They are people who see greater potential in us than we even see in ourselves. They call out the best in us. Often, they are coaches or teachers, but they can be friends or family.

....

Thank God today for someone who challenges or has challenged you to grow and push yourself. After your prayer, write an email, a text, or an actual letter to let the person know about your prayer of gratitude.

Friday, December 17

I am grateful to God, whom I worship with a clear conscience as my ancestors did, as I remember you constantly in my prayers, night and day. I yearn to see you again, recalling your tears, so that I may be filled with joy, as I recall your sincere faith.

—2 Timothy 1:3–5

Paul tells Timothy that he is grateful for him. He prays for Timothy constantly because of the close relationship they had. Paul mentored Timothy in the faith and was a spiritual father to him. They were like family.

....

Pray today for a family member or someone very close to you. Thank God today for the relationship you have with him or her. After your prayer, write an email, a text, or an actual letter to let the person know about your prayer of gratitude.

Saturday, December 18

Psalm 80:2ac, 3b, 15–16, 18–19

Lord, make us turn to you; let us see your face and we shall be saved.

O shepherd of Israel, hearken,
From your throne upon the cherubim, shine forth.
Rouse your power.

Lord, make us turn to you; let us see your face and we shall be saved.

Once again, O LORD of hosts,
look down from heaven, and see;
Take care of this vine,
and protect what your right hand has planted
the son of man whom you yourself made strong.

Lord, make us turn to you; let us see your face and we shall be saved.

May your help be with the man of your right hand,
with the son of man whom you yourself made
        strong.
Then we will no more withdraw from you;
give us new life, and we will call upon your name.

Lord, make us turn to you; let us see your face and we shall be saved.

FOURTH WEEK

OF ADVENT

Sunday, December 19

The passage from Luke's gospel for the fourth Sunday of Advent shows an excellent example of gratitude in the story of the Visitation. Mary, after learning she is to be the Mother of the Messiah, visits her cousin Elizabeth who is six months pregnant.

Mary expresses her gratitude by visiting Elizabeth. Mary not only gives the gift of her presence but also brings Jesus to her cousin, since she carries him inside her. In the same way, we can show our gratitude to God when we bring Jesus into our interactions with others, especially people who don't know Jesus.

....

Pray today for the grace to be like Mary. Pray that you will bring Jesus into all your relationships and interactions with others today.

Monday, December 20

[John the Baptist] said to the crowds who came out to be baptized by him, . . . "Produce good fruits as evidence of your repentance; and do not begin to say to yourselves, 'We have Abraham as our father,' for I tell you, God can raise up children to Abraham from these stones."

—Luke 3:7a, 8

Before Jesus' ministry, John the Baptist prepared the way by his preaching and teaching. Crowds of people came to hear him speak and to be baptized by him. He told the people that in order to prepare the way to recognize the Messiah, they had to act. It wasn't enough to rest on their heritage. They had to produce good fruit as evidence that they were turning toward God.

While good deeds do not earn God's love or grace, they do help us to recognize God. Giving and good deeds are ways in which we turn our attention toward God and prepare the way for him to come into our hearts.

....

Ask the Holy Spirit to help you recognize one or two opportunities to do good today—to give your time, talent, or treasure to others.

Tuesday, December 21

And the crowds asked him, "What then should we do?" He said to them in reply, "Whoever has two tunics should share with the person who has none. And whoever has food should do likewise."
—Luke 3:10–11

The crowds of people respond positively to John the Baptist. They want to produce good works as a sign of repentance. They want to prepare the way for the Messiah so they can recognize him. So, they ask a simple question, "What should we do?" John tells them to give away their extra—to share.

At this time of the year, we are predisposed to giving and sharing our extra. You may well have plenty of extra: extra food, clothes, and money that you don't absolutely need. God wants us to recognize our extra not so we feel guilty but so we feel grateful. Then, out of gratitude to him, we share our resources with people who have little or none. Even those who have little by way of material goods can often find ways to give to those in need. Is there a neighbor who can use help or simply a visit? Is there a lonely child who can use a friend?

....

Thank God today for the extra you have and find ways to share with those who need your abundance.

Wednesday, December 22

Then the king will say to those on his right, "Come, you who are blessed by my Father. Inherit the kingdom prepared for you from the foundation of the world. For I was hungry and you gave me food, I was thirsty and you gave me drink, a stranger and you welcomed me, naked and you clothed me, ill and you cared for me, in prison and you visited me. . . . Whatever you did for one of the least brothers of mine, you did for me."

—Matthew 25:34–36, 40

Jesus describes the end of time. When he comes to judge the heavens and the earth, he will separate people into two groups. On the one side will be people who have given to others and on the other side those who have not. Jesus tells the group that has given to others that whenever they gave food or drink or welcoming or the gift of their presence to others, they did it for him.

When we are grateful for someone, we often give them a gift as an expression of our gratitude. We send flowers or give some token of our appreciation. We thank God when we give and share what we have with the least resourced of our brothers and sisters.

....

Pray today for the grace to recognize opportunities to give to people in need. Ask for the grace to express your gratitude to God by giving.

Thursday, December 23

How can I repay the LORD for all the great good done for me? . . . I will offer a sacrifice of praise and call on the name of the LORD. I will pay my vows to the LORD in the presence of all his people, In the courts of the house of the LORD, in your midst, O Jerusalem. Hallelujah!

—Psalm 116:12, 17–19

The psalmist asks a great question: how can I thank God for his goodness and mercy? The psalm lists a few ways to thank God for his goodness. Here he describes financial giving as an expression of gratitude.

He says that he will offer a sacrifice of thanksgiving. He will sacrifice an animal, which would have been a financial offering at that time. He says he will "pay his vows to the Lord" in the presence of God's people. In other words, when he is at worship, he will give. Thanks and giving go together.

....

Thank God today that you have resources to give back to him and to give to others. The next time you give, thank God that you get to give as an expression of gratitude.

Friday, December 24

When Elizabeth heard Mary's greeting, the infant leaped in her womb, and Elizabeth, filled with the Holy Spirit, cried out in a loud voice and said, "Most blessed are you among women, and blessed is the fruit of your womb. And how does this happen to me, that the mother of my Lord should come to me?"

—Luke 1:41–43

Mary goes to visit Elizabeth and serve her in her pregnancy. Elizabeth responds with gratitude for Mary's visit. She asks, "How does this happen to me, that the mother of my Lord should come to me?" She is humbled that Mary would give of her time to be with her.

Humility precedes gratitude. While entitlement prevents us from recognizing our blessings, humility opens our eyes to see our gifts. When we do not think so much of ourselves that we deserve a gift, but rather are humbled that others would even think of us, gratitude follows.

....

In these final hours of Advent, read the words of Elizabeth again. Repeat those words in prayer. How does it happen that God sent his Son into the world for me? How does it happen that God thinks so much of me that he sent his Son to die for me?

CHRISTMASTIME

Saturday, December 25
The Nativity of the Lord

In those days a decree went out from Caesar Augustus that the whole world should be enrolled. . . . So all went to be enrolled, each to his own town. And Joseph too went up . . . to Judea, to the city of David that is called Bethlehem, because he was of the house and family of David, to be enrolled with Mary, his betrothed, who was with child. While they were there, the time came for her to have her child, and she gave birth to her firstborn son. She wrapped him in swaddling clothes and laid him in a manger, because there was no room for them in the inn.

—Luke 2:1, 3–7

As the result of a decree from Caesar, Joseph and Mary leave their town of Nazareth. They make a long and arduous journey to go to Bethlehem, which means "house of bread." This fulfills the prophecy from Micah that the Messiah would come from Bethlehem.

In Bethlehem, Mary gives birth to Jesus. She goes through the pain of labor. The Son of God had to go through the process of birth and all that entails. Joseph had to struggle with being unable to provide a room for his family. The birth of our Savior is a beautiful event, as well as one of great sacrifice.

....

On this Christmas morning, imagine yourself at the scene of the Nativity. Express your gratitude for the sacrifice of Jesus, Mary, and Joseph.

Sunday, December 26

Now there were shepherds in that region living in the fields and keeping the night watch over their flock. The angel of the Lord appeared to them and the glory of the Lord shone around them, and they were struck with great fear. The angel said to them, "Do not be afraid; for behold, I proclaim to you good news of great joy that will be for all the people."

—Luke 2:8–10

God had given the greatest gift when he sent his Son into the world. However, no one recognized this gift. The gift was made known to shepherds who were watching their flock by night. The angels appeared to the shepherds and told them they were bringing good news of great joy for all people. This means it is good news for each and every person. It is good news for you.

As human beings, it is so easy to take our gifts for granted. We fail to recognize and see them. We need angels or messengers to help us recognize our blessings. We need to be reminded over and over again of the greatest gift we have in the person of Jesus Christ. His coming into the world is good news of great joy.

....

Thank God today for the gift of his Son. Thank God that he has given you the gospels and his Church to remind you of that blessing.

Monday, December 27

The angel said to them, "Do not be afraid; for behold, I proclaim to you good news of great joy that will be for all the people. For today in the city of David a savior has been born for you who is Messiah and Lord. And this will be a sign for you: you will find an infant wrapped in swaddling clothes and lying in a manger."

—Luke 2:10–12

The angels tell the shepherds not to be afraid because they bring good news. They bring good news of great joy because a savior has been born. They tell the shepherds how they can recognize their savior—he will be wrapped in swaddling clothes and lying in a manger.

The gift of Jesus is the gift of a Savior. That can sound a bit offensive. Needing a Savior implies that we don't have it all together, that we need help. However, just a little reflection and a little dose of reality can remind us that we all need saving from bitterness, anger, ingratitude, self-centeredness, fear, guilt, and pride. These are human problems that cannot be solved with human solutions. We need a divine Savior who is Christ and Lord.

....

Today, thank Jesus that he is your Savior.

Tuesday, December 28

When the angels went away from them to heaven, the shepherds said to one another, "Let us go, then, to Bethlehem to see this thing that has taken place, which the Lord has made known to us." So they went in haste and found Mary and Joseph, and the infant lying in the manger. When they saw this, they made known the message that had been told them about this child. All who heard it were amazed by what had been told them by the shepherds. And Mary kept all these things, reflecting on them in her heart. Then the shepherds returned, glorifying and praising God for all they had heard and seen, just as it had been told to them.

—Luke 2:15–20

The angels make the shepherds aware of the great gift of the Savior. The shepherds receive the news and recognize the gift. They then turn their attention toward the gift and the giver of the gift. They make haste to go to Bethlehem and share their story with Mary. They then thank God for the gift by praising him for what they have heard and seen.

Praise is a great way to express our gratitude to God. Praise God today for the gift of his Son. Praise him for all that you have seen and heard about him.

Wednesday, December 29

[Simeon] came in the Spirit into the temple; and when the parents brought in the child Jesus to perform the custom of the law in regard to him, he took him into his arms and blessed God, saying: "Now, Master, you may let your servant go in peace, according to your word, for my eyes have seen your salvation."

—Luke 2:27–30

Luke tells us that Simeon was a devout and righteous man, long awaiting the restoration of God's rule in Israel. When Mary and Joseph present Jesus to the Lord in the temple, they meet Simeon, who takes Jesus into his arms and recognizes in the child, the one promised, the Messiah who was save his people.

Even the blessings of this busy season can feel like a burden if we don't stop to recognize them, turn our attention to God, and express our gratitude. Simeon knew to bless or thank God for a promised fulfilled.

We can express gratitude to God by slowing down to call to mind our blessings, our hope for salvation upon which we depend to see us through even the toughest times of our lives.

....

Today, ask God to teach you to self-reflection, to show you the hope of salvation, and spark within you the desire to give generously in a spirit of gratitude for the blessings of your life.

Thursday, December 30

There was also a prophetess, Anna, the daughter of Phanuel, of the tribe of Asher. She was advanced in years, having lived seven years with her husband after her marriage, and then as a widow until she was eighty-four. She never left the temple, but worshiped night and day with fasting and prayer. And coming forward at that very time, she gave thanks to God and spoke about the child to all who were awaiting the redemption of Jerusalem.

—Luke 2:36–38

Imagine spending a lifetime bound to one place, giving your days over to God in fasting and prayer. Imagine how much more you might notice God at work in the world. Imagine how it would be to see Christ and immediately know him as Anna did.

....

This is an excellent time to find a quiet place and look back on the blessings of the past year and recognize them with words of praise and gratitude to God.

Friday, December 31

In the beginning was the Word, and the Word was with God, and the Word was God. He was in the beginning with God. All things came to be through him, and without him nothing came to be. What came to be through him was life, and this life was the light of the human race; the light shines in the darkness, and the darkness does not overcome it.
—John 1:1–5

The Gospel of John introduces Jesus not through the Nativity scenes, but as the eternal Word of God. Everything that exists came to be because of him. We have life because of Jesus.

Take a few minutes to reflect on the blessings of your life this past year where you were just happy to be alive. What were some of the events or moments that brought joy to your heart? You may want to think about travel or a vacation, times with family, or getting to enjoy a favorite hobby.

On this last day of the year, make a list of the blessings of the past year and then thank God for each of those blessings.

Saturday, January 1
Solemnity of
Mary, the Holy Mother of God

So they went in haste and found Mary and Joseph, and the infant lying in the manger. When they saw this, they made known the message that had been told them about this child. All who heard it were amazed by what had been told them by the shepherds. And Mary kept all these things, reflecting on them in her heart.

—Luke 2:16–19

After the angels announce the birth of Jesus, the shepherds go to Bethlehem to see the child. They recount their experience and all were amazed, but Mary does something more. She reflects on the events in her heart. She savors these events.

....

Reflect again on the blessings of the past year. You may want to add to your list people to whom you have grown closer this year or new friendships that have formed. Savor the blessings. Turn them over in your heart as if you are looking at a diamond or other precious jewel from different angles. Thank God for those blessings.

Sunday, January 2
Solemnity of the Epiphany

> And this is the testimony of John. When the Jews from Jerusalem sent priests and Levites [to him] to ask him, "Who are you?" he admitted and did not deny it, but admitted, "I am not the Messiah." So they asked him, "What are you then? Are you Elijah?" And he said, "I am not." "Are you the Prophet?" He answered, "No." So they said to him, "Who are you, so we can give an answer to those who sent us?" . . . He said: "I am 'the voice of one crying out in the desert, "Make straight the way of the Lord,"' as Isaiah the prophet said."
>
> —John 1:19–23

John the Baptist drew crowds of people even though he preached away from the religious center of Jerusalem. The religious leaders sent emissaries to find out who John was and whether he might think he was the Messiah. John says he is not the Messiah, he is not Elijah, and he is not the prophet. Finally, the representatives of the religious leaders ask John to describe who he is. John references a verse from Isaiah, which describes how he sees himself and his mission.

In the year 2022 and in the years ahead, God has a mission for you: something he wants to do through you that he will not do through another.

....

Thank God today that he has a mission for you. Ask God to help show you that mission as well. You may even want to pray for him to give you a verse from scripture that describes your identity and mission just as he did with John the Baptist.

Monday, January 3

See what love the Father has bestowed on us that we may be called the children of God. Yet so we are. The reason the world does not know us is that it did not know him. Beloved, we are God's children now; what we shall be has not yet been revealed. We do know that when it is revealed we shall be like him, for we shall see him as he is.

—1 John 3:1–2

John reminds us of the blessing of God's great love for us. God gives us life; he creates us and then calls us his children. We are sons and daughters of God—that is our identity through our baptism. God's love for us is a firm foundation. Since we are God's children, he calls us to become more like him. In the coming year, God wants you to reflect his character more and more.

....

Thank God today that he is transforming your character to be like his. Ask God to show you one way he wants you to be more like him in the year ahead. Pray for the wisdom to know how you can cooperate with that transformation.

Tuesday, January 4

Andrew, the brother of Simon Peter, was one of the two who heard John and followed Jesus. He first found his brother Simon and told him, "We have found the Messiah" (which is translated Anointed). Then he brought him to Jesus. Jesus looked at him and said, "You are Simon the son of John; you will be called Cephas" (which is translated Peter).

—John 1:40–42

Andrew brings his brother Simon to meet Jesus because he believes Jesus is the Messiah. When Jesus sees Simon he gives him a new name. He calls him "Cephas," which means huge rock. Jesus identifies Peter as the rock, the solid foundation of the Church.

Like Peter, Jesus has a name for us. He sees something in us that we might not see in ourselves. Only Jesus can give us our name because we belong to him. He calls us always to keep becoming more conformed to who he is, to be more and more like him in all things.

....

Thank Jesus today that he alone can give you your name, your deepest identity. Ask him who he wants you to be.

Wednesday, January 5

Give and gifts will be given to you; a good measure, packed together, shaken down, and overflowing, will be poured into your lap. For the measure with which you measure will in return be measured out to you.

—Luke 6:38

Jesus tells us that when we give, we open ourselves to God's blessing. He uses the image of people being at a market. To make sure someone was getting their money's worth, grain would be shaken to show it was a fair amount for the money given. Jesus says that when we give, we receive back from God—except we don't get what we have given, we receive an abundance more that is overflowing.

We give to God as a sign of our gratitude, but we cannot out-give God. As St. Ignatius of Loyola noted, we will sooner tire of receiving God's gifts and blessing than he will of giving to us. Giving and gratitude open us up to more of God's blessing.

....

Thank God today for the abundance he has given you.

Thursday, January 6
The Traditional Date of Epiphany

When Jesus was born in Bethlehem of Judea, in the days of King Herod, behold, magi from the east arrived in Jerusalem, saying, "Where is the new-born king of the Jews? We saw his star at its rising and have come to do him homage." When King Herod heard this, he was greatly troubled, and all Jerusalem with him.

—Matthew 2:1–3

Consider why Herod and the other leaders of Jerusalem would fear a newborn, whom some were already calling "king." Their power was threatened of course—both political and religious power. We know from later in Matthew's gospel that Herod ordered the massacre of all male children two years old and younger in Bethlehem and the surrounding area because he felt so threatened.

Sometimes our place in life, at work or school, in our families, neighborhoods, or churches, can seem threatened. At times our fear of losing our power causes us to hoard information or spread rumors about those who might threaten us. At other times, we lie or cheat to retain power. But Jesus came as a powerless infant, utterly dependent, and died crucified, stripped of all worldly power.

....

Today, thank God for your places of power, well-being, and safety in this world. Ask Jesus to be your guide in not clinging to that power but sharing what you are able of it with a kind and generous spirit.

Fr. Michael White is a priest of the Archdiocese of Baltimore and pastor of Church of the Nativity in Timonium, Maryland. White is the coauthor of *Rebuilt*—which narrates the story of Nativity's rebirth—*Tools for Rebuilding, Rebuilding Your Message, The Rebuilt Field Guide*, and *ChurchMoney*. He is also coauthor of the bestselling Messages series for Advent and Lent.

During White's tenure as pastor at Church of the Nativity, the church has almost tripled in weekend attendance. More importantly, commitment to the mission of the Church has grown, demonstrated by the significant increase of giving and service in ministry, and much evidence of genuine spiritual renewal.

White earned his bachelor's degree from Loyola University Maryland and his graduate degrees in sacred theology and ecclesiology from the Pontifical Gregorian University in Rome.

Tom Corcoran has served Church of the Nativity in Timonium, Maryland, in a variety of roles that give him a unique perspective on parish ministry and leadership. First hired as a youth minister, Corcoran has also served as coordinator of children's ministry and director of small groups. He is lay associate to the pastor and is responsible for weekend message development, strategic planning, and staff development.

Corcoran is the coauthor of *Rebuilt*—which narrates the story of Nativity's rebirth—*Tools for Rebuilding, Rebuilding Your Message, The Rebuilt Field Guide*, and *ChurchMoney*. He is also coauthor of the bestselling Messages series for Advent and Lent.

churchnativity.com
rebuiltparish.com

rebuiltparish.podbean.com
Facebook: churchnativity
Twitter: @churchnativity
Instagram: @churchnativity